WhatsApp Evolution and Digital Responsibility

C. P. Kumar
Reiki Healer
Roorkee - 247667, India

Disclaimer

While every effort has been made to ensure the accuracy and completeness of the content in this book, the author cannot guarantee that the information contained herein is error-free, up-to-date, or suitable for every individual circumstance.

The author shall not be held liable or responsible for any errors or omissions in the content of the book, nor for any damages, or losses that may arise from any actions taken based upon the suggestions or contents presented in the book.

Readers are advised to use their own judgment and discretion in applying the information provided in this book, and to consult with qualified professionals before taking any action based on the contents of this book. The author disclaims any and all liability or responsibility for any actions taken or not taken based on the information contained in this book.

DEDICATION

To all those who embrace the digital realm with a profound sense of responsibility, understanding that the evolution of technology carries both the power to connect and the responsibility to safeguard the bonds that unite us. May this exploration of WhatsApp's journey and its impact on our lives inspire a generation committed to shaping a digital future anchored in empathy, wisdom, and conscientious connectivity.

Your dedication to understanding, questioning, and nurturing the digital spaces we inhabit is the driving force behind the transformation of technology from a tool to a force for positive change. As we traverse the chapters of this book, may you find insight, inspiration, and the tools to shape a future where digital evolution and responsibility walk hand in hand.

C. P. Kumar

CONTENTS

Copyright 2

Disclaimer 3

DEDICATION 4

PREFACE 7

Chapter 1.   The Evolution of Communication Platforms 10

Chapter 2.   Instant Communication Revolution 15

Chapter 3.   Breaking Down Borders................................20

Chapter 4.   Economic Impact 24

Chapter 5.   Digital Dependency....................................28

Chapter 6.   The Misinformation Conundrum 32

Chapter 7.   Privacy in the Digital Age............................36

Chapter 8.   Group Dynamics and Social Identity 40

Chapter 9.   Addressing Hate Speech 44

Chapter 10.   Security and Vulnerabilities 48

Chapter 11.   Digital Literacy and Critical Thinking 53

Chapter 12.   Cultivating Healthy Online Habits....................58

Chapter 13.   Building Inclusive Communities......................62

Chapter 14.   Promoting Fact-Checking and Accuracy............67

Chapter 15.   Technological Trends and Innovations 71

Chapter 16.	Regulation and Governance 77

Chapter 17.	Ethical Design and User-Centricity....................82

Chapter 18.	Toward Digital Responsibility 87

PREFACE

In an era where the digital landscape is rapidly evolving, communication has transcended its traditional boundaries, ushering in an unprecedented era of connectivity and interaction. At the forefront of this transformative journey stands WhatsApp, a platform that has not only redefined the way we communicate but has also underscored the critical need for digital responsibility.

The book, "WhatsApp Evolution and Digital Responsibility," embarks on a comprehensive exploration of WhatsApp's evolution and its profound impact on our world. It delves deep into the intricacies of instant messaging, the socio-economic implications of this technology, and the ethical considerations that accompany it. Through a meticulous examination of the platform's evolution and its role in shaping modern communication dynamics, this book aims to unravel the intricate web of opportunities and challenges that WhatsApp presents.

As we navigate the chapters that follow, readers will traverse the historical tapestry of communication platforms, tracing their evolution from antiquity to the digital age. The story unfolds, leading us to the inception of WhatsApp and the remarkable paradigm shift it initiated. We investigate its contribution to breaking down geographical barriers, creating a world where borders are no longer constraints to connections.

An exploration of the economic impact of WhatsApp beckons, shedding light on its disruptive role in global economies and challenging conventional communication models. The book further delves into the psychological and social repercussions of digital dependency, unearthing the delicate balance between connectivity and well-being.

A pervasive issue, the spread of misinformation, is dissected with precision, revealing the complex interplay of technology, psychology, and society. In tandem, the multifaceted dimension of privacy is unveiled, inviting readers to contemplate encryption, data security, and the quest for user agency.

Navigating the intricate terrain of group dynamics and social identity, this book navigates the ways in which WhatsApp's group chats mold our perceptions and behaviors, for better or worse. Moreover, the discourse expands to tackle the ominous specter of hate speech, elucidating the challenges posed and proposing strategies for a safer digital realm.

Technical vulnerabilities and security breaches are scrutinized, highlighting the measures taken to safeguard user information. A clarion call for digital literacy and critical thinking resounds throughout the chapters, urging readers to become savvy consumers of information within the vast digital expanse.

As the narrative progresses, the spotlight turns toward cultivating healthy digital habits, building inclusive communities, and promoting fact-checking and accuracy. The trajectory of WhatsApp's technological journey is also charted, speculating on its integration with emerging innovations.

The intricate interplay of regulation and governance takes center stage, unraveling the dynamic relationship between governments and technology providers in the realm of digital communication. Ethical design principles emerge as a guiding light, propelling us toward a more responsible digital landscape.

Ultimately, the book culminates with a reflective summary, offering a comprehensive roadmap for responsible WhatsApp usage. It emphasizes the shared responsibility of individuals, technology providers, and society in shaping a digital realm that is both empowering and ethical.

In traversing the pages of "WhatsApp Evolution and Digital Responsibility," readers are invited to contemplate the fascinating journey of an app that has become synonymous with modern communication. Through insightful analysis, thought-provoking discussions, and pragmatic solutions, this book strives to illuminate both the potential and the pitfalls of WhatsApp, inspiring a collective commitment to digital responsibility in an interconnected world.

C. P. Kumar
Reiki Healer
Former Scientist 'G', National Institute of Hydrology
Roorkee - 247667, India
E-mail: cpkumar@yahoo.com
Web: https://www.angelfire.com/nh/cpkumar/virgo.html

Introduction

In today's rapidly evolving digital landscape, communication platforms have become an integral part of our daily lives. The way we interact, share information, and connect with others has undergone a remarkable transformation over the years. From the early days of telegraphs to the modern era of instant messaging, the evolution of communication platforms has been nothing short of revolutionary. This article delves into the historical context of communication technologies, leading up to the emergence of WhatsApp as a game-changer in the realm of digital communication.

The Dawn of Communication Technologies

The story of communication platforms can be traced back to the early innovations in telecommunication. In the 19th century, the invention of the telegraph marked a pivotal moment in human history. It allowed messages to be transmitted over long distances using electrical signals, effectively bridging the gap between distant locations. This breakthrough in communication laid the foundation for further advancements in the field.

Subsequently, the telephone emerged as another significant milestone. Alexander Graham Bell's invention of the telephone in 1876 revolutionized interpersonal communication, enabling real-time voice conversations between individuals separated by vast geographical distances. The telephone quickly became an essential part of businesses and households, reshaping societal interactions.

The Internet Revolution

The late 20th century witnessed a revolutionary development that would forever alter the way we communicate - the advent of the internet. The creation of the World Wide Web by Tim Berners-Lee in 1989 opened up unprecedented opportunities for global connectivity. Email became one of the first widely adopted digital communication platforms, allowing users to send written messages electronically.

As the internet continued to evolve, instant messaging platforms started to gain prominence. Services like ICQ and AOL Instant Messenger allowed users to exchange messages in real time, transcending the limitations of traditional email communication. These platforms laid the groundwork for the concept of instantaneity, which would later become a hallmark of modern communication platforms.

The Rise of Social Media

The early 2000s marked a significant shift in communication platforms with the rise of social media. Websites like Friendster, MySpace, and later Facebook transformed online interactions into social experiences, enabling users to connect, share updates, and communicate with friends and acquaintances on a global scale. These platforms blurred the lines between personal and digital identities, giving rise to a new era of interconnectedness.

In the midst of this social media boom, mobile phones were also undergoing a transformation. The introduction of smartphones brought about a paradigm shift in communication, as these devices combined telephony, internet access, and various applications in a single handheld device. Text messaging evolved into multimedia messaging, allowing users to share not only text but also photos, videos, and other media.

WhatsApp Emerges

Amidst this dynamic landscape, WhatsApp emerged as a true game-changer in the world of digital communication. Founded in 2009 by Brian Acton and Jan Koum, WhatsApp's journey began with a simple yet revolutionary idea - providing a platform for instant messaging using internet connectivity. This approach eliminated the need for traditional SMS messages, which often incurred additional charges, especially for international communication.

One of WhatsApp's key strengths was its user-friendly interface and seamless user experience. The app capitalized on the growing popularity of smartphones and the increasing availability of mobile internet, allowing users to exchange messages, make voice calls, and share media effortlessly. Its end-to-end encryption further bolstered its appeal, ensuring user privacy and security in an era of growing digital concerns.

WhatsApp's impact was felt across various demographics and regions, transcending barriers of age, geography, and culture. It became an essential tool for personal communication, business interactions, and even social activism. The platform's group chat feature facilitated efficient communication among groups of people, enabling coordination, collaboration, and community-building.

Digital Responsibility in the Age of WhatsApp

With great technological advancements come great responsibilities. As communication platforms like WhatsApp gained prominence, questions of digital responsibility, privacy, and security began to surface. The platform's end-to-end encryption, while a boon for user privacy, also posed challenges for law enforcement and national security agencies. Striking the right balance between individual privacy and societal safety became a critical point of discussion.

Additionally, the spread of misinformation and fake news on WhatsApp raised concerns about its role in shaping public discourse. The platform's encrypted nature made it difficult to monitor and curb the dissemination of false information, leading to instances of social unrest and even violence in some cases. This highlighted the need for digital literacy, critical thinking, and responsible online behavior to counter the negative aspects of unfettered communication.

The Future of Communication Platforms

As we peer into the future, it's clear that communication platforms will continue to evolve and shape our interactions. The integration of artificial intelligence and machine learning could enhance user experiences by providing personalized recommendations, real-time language translation, and advanced chatbot interactions. Virtual and augmented reality technologies might offer immersive communication experiences, bridging the gap between physical and digital presence.

Moreover, the ongoing debate about digital responsibility and privacy is likely to influence the direction of communication platforms. Striking a harmonious balance between innovation, user convenience, and ethical considerations will be crucial in shaping the next phase of digital communication.

Conclusion

The evolution of communication platforms is a testament to human ingenuity and our innate desire to connect with one another. From the telegraph to WhatsApp, each technological leap has brought us closer together, transforming the way we communicate and share information. WhatsApp's emergence as a game-changer underscores the power of innovation in reshaping societal norms and behaviors. As we navigate the intricacies of digital responsibility, let us embrace the opportunities and challenges presented by these platforms, ensuring that our digital interactions continue to enrich our lives while upholding the values that define us.

Introduction

In the digital age, where time and distance are no longer insurmountable barriers, the evolution of instant communication has revolutionized the way we connect and interact. At the forefront of this transformation stands WhatsApp – a messaging platform that has reshaped interpersonal relationships, business communications, and societal interactions. This article delves into the significance of instant messaging and how WhatsApp, through its evolution, has redefined communication paradigms, fostering both unprecedented connectivity and new dimensions of digital responsibility.

The Emergence of Instant Messaging

The concept of instant messaging traces its roots back to the early days of the internet, when text-based communication tools like IRC (Internet Relay Chat) and ICQ (I Seek You) gained popularity. However, it wasn't until the mobile revolution that instant messaging truly transformed communication. The rise of smartphones, coupled with the proliferation of mobile internet, laid the foundation for a new era of connectivity – one that bridged geographical gaps and allowed real-time conversations to occur effortlessly.

The WhatsApp Revolution

Amidst the plethora of messaging apps that emerged, WhatsApp emerged as a frontrunner, rapidly gaining momentum and acclaim. Founded by Brian Acton and Jan Koum in 2009, WhatsApp's success was attributed to its simplicity, reliability, and commitment to user privacy. With its end-to-end encryption, WhatsApp ensured that conversations remained private and secure, resonating with users who sought a safe haven for their digital communications.

Transforming Personal Connections

Instant messaging via platforms like WhatsApp profoundly impacted personal relationships. The days of waiting for letters or playing phone tag (frustrating cycle of missed calls and voicemails between individuals attempting to communicate) were over; people could now share thoughts, pictures, and experiences instantly, regardless of physical location. Families living continents apart could exchange pleasantries, and friends separated by time zones could keep their bonds alive through constant communication. The emotional distance that often accompanied physical separation was mitigated, creating a sense of togetherness that transcended borders.

Furthermore, WhatsApp introduced the notion of "status updates," allowing users to share glimpses of their lives with a wide circle of acquaintances. This innovation, while often seen as a minor feature, symbolized a shift in how people presented themselves digitally, contributing to the creation of a shared online narrative.

Revolutionizing Business Communications

Beyond personal connections, WhatsApp reshaped the business landscape. The platform's accessibility and user-friendly interface made it an ideal tool for businesses to communicate with customers, vendors, and partners. Small enterprises, especially in emerging economies, harnessed the power of WhatsApp to market their products, provide customer support, and facilitate transactions. This democratization of business communication leveled the playing field, enabling even modest enterprises to compete in the global marketplace.

WhatsApp Business, a derivative of the main platform, was launched to cater specifically to business needs. It offered features like automated responses and catalog display, streamlining customer interactions and enhancing overall user experience. This evolution not only facilitated seamless interactions but also paved the way for innovative business models that relied heavily on instant communication.

Social and Societal Impacts

The rise of instant messaging platforms, including WhatsApp, has given birth to new forms of digital socialization. Group chats, for instance, have become virtual meeting spaces where friends, family members, and colleagues can exchange ideas, plan events, and engage in casual banter. These digital communities foster a sense of belonging and camaraderie, albeit in a digital realm.

However, alongside the positive social impacts, instant messaging also introduced new challenges. The instant nature of communication sometimes led to misunderstandings, as nuances that are present in face-to-face interactions or longer-form written communication were lost in the brevity of text messages. Additionally, the constant connectivity that instant messaging enables has raised concerns about digital addiction and its potential impact on mental well-being.

Digital Responsibility in the WhatsApp Era

With great power comes great responsibility, and the era of instant messaging is no exception. As WhatsApp gained prominence, issues related to privacy, misinformation, and cyberbullying emerged. The end-to-end encryption that was lauded for its security features also posed challenges for law enforcement and national security agencies, sparking debates about striking the right balance between privacy and public safety.

Misinformation, often spread through forwarded messages, became a significant concern. The speed at which information travels on instant messaging platforms can lead to the rapid dissemination of false or misleading content. WhatsApp took steps to curb this by limiting the forwarding of messages and introducing labels to indicate messages that have been frequently forwarded. However, the battle against misinformation is ongoing, requiring a collaborative effort from technology companies, users, and society at large.

Cyberbullying and harassment, unfortunately, found a new avenue through instant messaging. The relative anonymity and immediacy offered by platforms like WhatsApp facilitated negative behaviors that could have lasting impacts on individuals. This highlighted the need for digital responsibility, emphasizing the importance of respectful communication and the ethical use of technology.

Conclusion

The evolution of instant messaging, with WhatsApp at its forefront, has undeniably transformed the way we connect, communicate, and interact. Personal relationships have been strengthened, business dynamics have evolved, and society has witnessed both positive and challenging outcomes. As we navigate this brave new world of instant communication, the concept of digital responsibility becomes ever more crucial. WhatsApp, while ushering in a new era of connectivity, reminds us that our actions in the digital realm carry real-world consequences – a reminder that is not just pertinent but imperative for the modern age.

Introduction

In the modern digital age, communication has evolved drastically, breaking down traditional barriers and redefining how we connect with one another. Among the myriad of tools that have facilitated this transformation, WhatsApp stands out as a powerful platform that has played a pivotal role in connecting people across geographical boundaries, fostering global interactions, and promoting a sense of unity in diversity. This article delves into the evolution of WhatsApp as a tool for breaking down borders and highlights its role in promoting digital responsibility.

The Genesis of Connectivity

WhatsApp, initially founded in 2009 by Brian Acton and Jan Koum, emerged as a solution to a simple yet profound challenge - staying connected with loved ones regardless of their location. This initial vision paved the way for WhatsApp's meteoric rise as a cross-platform messaging application, capable of transcending geographical and cultural differences. From its humble beginnings, WhatsApp evolved into a global communication powerhouse, connecting people irrespective of their physical location, and thus laying the foundation for breaking down borders.

Connecting Cultures

One of the most remarkable features of WhatsApp's evolution has been its ability to transcend language barriers. The platform offers support for numerous languages, enabling users from diverse linguistic backgrounds to communicate seamlessly. Through features like real-time translation and multilingual chat, WhatsApp facilitates interactions that were previously hindered by language differences.

In a world marked by cultural diversity, WhatsApp has become a virtual meeting ground where individuals can share their traditions, beliefs, and experiences. Whether it's a Chinese New Year greeting or an Indian Diwali celebration, WhatsApp allows people to connect with their roots, share their cultural practices, and gain a deeper understanding of the world's myriad traditions.

Global Commerce and Entrepreneurship

WhatsApp's impact is not limited to personal connections alone. The platform has also played a significant role in reshaping global commerce and entrepreneurship. Small and medium-sized businesses across the world have leveraged WhatsApp as a tool for marketing, customer engagement, and even conducting transactions. This has enabled entrepreneurs to break free from the confines of their local markets and engage with a global customer base.

By facilitating seamless communication between businesses and consumers, WhatsApp has empowered individuals to become global entrepreneurs, transcending geographical constraints and expanding their reach beyond borders. This evolution of commerce is not only reshaping economies but also contributing to a more interconnected world.

Crisis Communication and Social Change

WhatsApp's role in breaking down borders is especially evident during times of crisis and social change. The platform has been instrumental in disseminating critical information during natural disasters, political upheavals, and health emergencies. From providing real-time updates on disaster relief efforts to spreading awareness about public health measures, WhatsApp has emerged as a vital tool for crisis communication.

Furthermore, WhatsApp has facilitated social change by giving a voice to marginalized communities and enabling grassroots activism. Citizens from different corners of the world can come together, share their experiences, and collectively advocate for change. This newfound connectivity has the power to challenge oppressive regimes, raise awareness about social injustices, and amplify voices that were previously silenced by geographical boundaries.

Digital Responsibility

While WhatsApp's evolution has undeniably broken down geographical barriers, it also raises important questions about digital responsibility. In this era of unprecedented connectivity, individuals must navigate the digital landscape with care, considering the global impact of their words and actions. The viral spread of misinformation, the potential for cyberbullying, and the need to respect cultural differences highlight the importance of responsible digital communication.

WhatsApp, as a central player in the digital revolution, has taken steps to address these challenges. The platform has introduced features to curb the spread of false information, enable users to control who can add them to groups, and report abusive content. However, digital responsibility is a collective effort that requires users to be conscious of their interactions and contribute to a positive online environment.

The Future of Connection

As technology continues to advance and shape the way we interact, WhatsApp is poised to play an even more significant role in breaking down borders. With the integration of emerging technologies like augmented reality, artificial intelligence, and virtual reality, the platform has the potential to offer immersive cross-cultural experiences that redefine global connectivity.

Conclusion

WhatsApp's evolution from a simple messaging app to a global communication juggernaut exemplifies the power of technology to break down geographical barriers and foster meaningful global connections. Through language diversity, cross-border commerce, crisis communication, and social change, WhatsApp has demonstrated its ability to transcend borders and unite people from all walks of life. However, this evolution also underscores the importance of digital responsibility, urging users to wield the platform's capabilities thoughtfully and contribute to a more inclusive and interconnected world. As we step into the future, WhatsApp's journey reminds us that the boundaries that once separated us are now merely lines on a digital map, waiting to be crossed with the touch of a screen.

Introduction

In today's rapidly evolving digital landscape, communication has undergone a paradigm shift, transforming the way individuals, businesses, and societies interact. One noteworthy catalyst for this transformation is WhatsApp, a cost-effective messaging system that has not only revolutionized the way we communicate but also left an indelible mark on traditional communication models and global economies. This article delves into the economic impact of WhatsApp's evolution, exploring its role in reshaping communication paradigms and its far-reaching consequences on global economic systems.

The inception of WhatsApp in 2009 marked a turning point in the communication sphere. With its user-friendly interface and ability to send text, images, videos, and audio messages over the internet, WhatsApp quickly gained traction. The app's cost-effectiveness, fueled by its utilization of data networks rather than traditional cellular networks, led to a dramatic reduction in communication expenses for individuals and businesses alike. As a result, the economic dynamics of communication began to shift, influencing both established communication models and larger economic frameworks.

Disruption of Traditional Communication Models

One of the most profound impacts of WhatsApp's evolution is the disruption it caused to traditional communication models. Historically, communication relied heavily on landline phones, mobile calls, and SMS services. These methods often incurred substantial costs, especially for international communication. WhatsApp's introduction of internet-based messaging undercut these costs, enabling users to send messages and make calls at a fraction of the traditional rates. This shift significantly altered consumer behavior, as individuals and businesses increasingly turned to WhatsApp as their primary mode of communication.

Moreover, WhatsApp's multimedia capabilities fostered a richer communication experience, allowing users to share information in diverse formats. This evolution led to a decline in the demand for traditional voice calls and SMS, impacting the revenues of telecommunication companies that had long thrived on these services. As users gravitated toward the cost-effective alternatives offered by WhatsApp, telecommunication companies were forced to reevaluate their business models, invest in data networks, and explore new avenues for revenue generation.

Global Economic Implications

The economic impact of WhatsApp's evolution transcended individual communication preferences, extending to influence global economies. As more users embraced WhatsApp, the reduced reliance on traditional communication channels resulted in a considerable decrease in global telecommunication revenue. While this shift was a boon for consumers, it presented challenges for telecommunication companies and governments that heavily relied on communication-related revenue streams.

On a macroeconomic level, the reduced communication expenses offered by WhatsApp translated into increased disposable income for individuals. As communication costs diminished, people had more resources to allocate to other goods and services, thereby driving demand in various sectors. This economic stimulus, albeit indirect, contributed to the growth and diversification of economies, fostering job creation and entrepreneurship.

WhatsApp's Role in Business Communication

Businesses also reaped the benefits of WhatsApp's cost-effective messaging system. Small and medium-sized enterprises (SMEs), in particular, leveraged the platform to connect with customers, manage inquiries, and facilitate transactions. The app's features, such as group chats and broadcast lists, enabled businesses to engage with a broader audience while minimizing costs. This shift in communication dynamics allowed SMEs to compete on a more level playing field with larger corporations, spurring innovation and competition within industries.

Additionally, WhatsApp's integration of business-specific tools further catalyzed its role in commerce. Features like WhatsApp Business API and catalog integration enabled businesses to create a seamless shopping experience within the app, blurring the lines between communication and e-commerce. This convergence not only streamlined operations but also influenced consumer behavior, as individuals increasingly turned to WhatsApp not only for communication but also for product discovery and purchasing.

Challenges and Considerations

While WhatsApp's economic impact has been largely positive, it has also raised certain challenges and considerations. The app's reliance on internet connectivity means that regions with limited or unstable internet access may not fully enjoy its benefits. This digital divide underscores the importance of continued efforts to expand internet infrastructure and ensure equitable access to communication tools.

Moreover, the rapid proliferation of WhatsApp as a communication channel has prompted concerns related to privacy and data security. The app's end-to-end encryption, while enhancing privacy, has also raised questions about potential misuse for illicit activities. As governments and regulatory bodies grapple with these issues, finding a balance between individual privacy and collective security remains a pressing challenge.

Conclusion

The evolution of WhatsApp from a simple messaging app to a multifaceted communication and commerce platform has had a profound economic impact on both traditional communication models and global economies. Its cost-effective nature disrupted established communication channels, altering consumer behavior and influencing telecommunication revenue streams. At the same time, WhatsApp's role in business communication has empowered SMEs and transformed the dynamics of commerce.

As we navigate the ever-changing digital landscape, understanding the economic implications of platforms like WhatsApp is crucial. The app's ability to reduce communication costs, foster economic growth, and shape the way businesses engage with customers highlights its significance in the broader context of digital responsibility. Balancing the advantages of cost-effective communication with the challenges of privacy and data security will ultimately determine how societies harness the economic potential of platforms like WhatsApp while safeguarding individual and collective interests.

Introduction

In an era marked by unprecedented technological advancement, the pervasive presence of digital platforms like WhatsApp has transformed the way we communicate and interact with the world around us. As we delve deeper into the age of information and instant communication, it becomes increasingly crucial to examine the phenomenon of digital dependency. This article aims to delve into the psychological effects of constant connectivity, shedding light on its implications for personal well-being and relationships.

The Allure of Instant Connectivity

The evolution of communication technology has brought about a significant shift in how we connect with others. WhatsApp, a trailblazer in this field, has redefined interpersonal communication by offering instantaneous messaging, multimedia sharing, and group interactions. This instantaneity has become a double-edged sword, offering convenience and connection on one hand, while potentially leading to digital dependency on the other.

The Psychological Toll of Constant Connectivity

While the benefits of staying connected through platforms like WhatsApp are undeniable, research has highlighted the potential psychological toll of constant connectivity. One of the key aspects to consider is the detrimental impact on mental well-being. The incessant notifications, the compulsion to respond promptly, and the fear of missing out can contribute to heightened stress levels, anxiety, and even burnout.

The Dopamine Dilemma

The instant gratification provided by digital interactions triggers the release of dopamine, a neurotransmitter associated with pleasure and reward. This neurological response creates a cycle of seeking validation and satisfaction through constant digital engagement. Over time, this can pave the way for addictive behaviors, making individuals more prone to checking their devices compulsively.

Impact on Personal Relationships

The rise of digital dependency has not only influenced individual well-being but also posed challenges to personal relationships. While platforms like WhatsApp enable us to stay connected across distances, they can inadvertently lead to a sense of disconnection in face-to-face interactions. The constant presence of devices during social interactions can lead to decreased engagement, hindered emotional connection, and a diminished sense of presence.

The Illusion of Connection

Digital communication often creates an illusion of intimacy. The ability to share personal moments, thoughts, and emotions through text and multimedia can foster a false sense of closeness. However, this superficial connection may lack the depth and nuance of in-person interactions, potentially leaving individuals feeling isolated and misunderstood.

Fostering Digital Responsibility

Acknowledging the psychological effects of constant connectivity is the first step towards fostering digital responsibility. This entails a mindful and balanced approach to digital engagement. Setting boundaries, such as designated device-free times or tech-free zones, can help create space for genuine human connection and reduce the adverse psychological impact of digital dependency.

Cultivating Mindfulness in the Digital Age

Mindfulness, with its emphasis on being fully present in the moment, can serve as a powerful antidote to digital dependency. Integrating mindfulness practices into daily routines can enhance self-awareness, reduce reactivity to notifications, and promote a healthier relationship with technology. Mindfulness encourages individuals to focus on real-world interactions and cultivate meaningful connections.

Promoting Digital Detox

Periodic digital detoxes can play a pivotal role in breaking the cycle of digital dependency. Temporarily disconnecting from digital platforms allows individuals to recalibrate their relationship with technology, reassess priorities, and reconnect with themselves and their surroundings. Digital detoxes provide an opportunity to appreciate the richness of offline experiences and foster genuine human interactions.

Nurturing Authentic Connections

While digital communication is a valuable tool, nurturing authentic connections requires deliberate effort. Engaging in face-to-face interactions, active listening, and non-verbal cues contribute to meaningful relationships. Balancing digital communication with in-person interactions can help bridge the gap between the virtual and physical worlds.

Educating for Digital Literacy

To mitigate the negative psychological effects of constant connectivity, promoting digital literacy is essential. Educating individuals about the psychological dynamics of digital platforms empowers them to make informed choices about their digital interactions. Understanding the persuasive design elements, such as notifications and social validation, can help individuals regain control over their online experiences.

Conclusion

The evolution of WhatsApp and similar digital platforms has undeniably transformed the way we connect and communicate. While the benefits are immense, it is crucial to navigate the digital landscape with mindfulness and responsibility. Constant connectivity has the potential to foster digital dependency, impacting personal well-being and relationships. By fostering digital responsibility, practicing mindfulness, embracing digital detoxes, and nurturing authentic connections, we can harness the power of digital platforms while safeguarding our mental and emotional well-being in the ever-evolving digital age.

Introduction

In the rapidly evolving digital landscape, social media platforms like WhatsApp have redefined the way we communicate and share information. The power to connect with people across the globe in an instant has transformed our lives, but it has also given rise to a complex challenge - the spread of misinformation. This article delves deep into the mechanisms behind the rampant dissemination of false information on WhatsApp and its far-reaching consequences on society, emphasizing the need for digital responsibility.

The Whispering Web: Mechanisms of Misinformation

1. Instant Gratification and Virality

In the age of information overload, the human psyche seeks instant gratification and validation. WhatsApp's design, with its ability to instantly share messages, images, and videos, plays into this inherent need. Content that triggers emotions such as fear, anger, or excitement tends to spread faster, as recipients are compelled to forward it to others. Viral messages gain momentum, often without being critically assessed for accuracy.

2. Confirmation Bias and Echo Chambers

People tend to seek information that aligns with their existing beliefs and opinions, a phenomenon known as confirmation bias. WhatsApp groups, often consisting of like-minded individuals, create echo chambers where misinformation can thrive. When group members share and reinforce misinformation, it solidifies the false narrative within that closed circle.

3. Lack of Source Verification

In the race to share breaking news or sensational stories, individuals often neglect source verification. WhatsApp's encrypted nature makes it difficult to trace the origin of a message, making it easier for misinformation to be disguised as credible information. This lack of accountability amplifies the spread of false content.

Unraveling the Web: Consequences of Misinformation

1. Undermining Trust in Information

The widespread dissemination of false information erodes the public's trust in reliable sources. When misinformation is unknowingly shared by friends and family, it gains an air of credibility, further blurring the lines between truth and fiction. As trust in information wanes, society becomes susceptible to manipulation.

2. Health and Safety Risks

Misinformation on WhatsApp often extends to health-related topics, leading to dangerous consequences. Fake medical advice, misleading remedies, and inaccurate COVID-19 information have led people down perilous paths. In extreme cases, the spread of misinformation has resulted in avoidable health crises and loss of life.

3. Social and Political Polarization

Misinformation can exacerbate social divisions and political polarization. When divisive or false narratives are perpetuated through WhatsApp, they can deepen existing fault lines within societies. Manipulative actors exploit these divisions to advance their agendas, sowing discord and undermining social cohesion.

4. Economic Ramifications

Businesses and economies can suffer when misinformation spreads unchecked. False reports about products, services, or financial markets can lead to panic buying, stock market fluctuations, and damage to brand reputation. The economic consequences of misinformation ripple through industries and markets.

Navigating the Digital Responsibility Maze

1. Promoting Media Literacy

Education is a key tool in combating the misinformation conundrum. Promoting media literacy empowers individuals to critically assess information, distinguish between credible and unreliable sources, and identify common tactics used to spread misinformation.

2. Strengthening Platform Regulations

Social media platforms like WhatsApp must play an active role in curbing the spread of misinformation. Implementing stricter regulations, enhancing content moderation, and providing users with tools to report false information can help create a safer digital environment.

3. Encouraging Responsible Sharing

Individuals have a vital role in breaking the cycle of misinformation. Encouraging responsible sharing involves verifying information before forwarding it, engaging in respectful conversations, and being mindful of the potential consequences of their actions.

4. Fostering Critical Thinking

Critical thinking skills are essential in the digital age. Schools, institutions, and communities should prioritize teaching individuals how to evaluate information critically, question sources, and make informed decisions based on evidence.

Conclusion

The evolution of WhatsApp and the broader digital landscape has undeniably revolutionized communication, but it has also exposed us to the dark underbelly of misinformation. Understanding the mechanisms that facilitate the spread of false information is the first step towards combating this formidable challenge. The consequences of misinformation are far-reaching, affecting our trust in information, public health, social fabric, and economies.

As we move forward, it is imperative that we embrace digital responsibility. By promoting media literacy, encouraging responsible sharing, fostering critical thinking, and holding platforms accountable, we can collectively navigate the intricate web of misinformation. The path to a more informed and resilient society begins with our willingness to challenge falsehoods, seek truth, and engage in thoughtful discourse. In the evolving landscape of WhatsApp and beyond, our commitment to digital responsibility will shape the future of information dissemination and ensure a more transparent, connected, and trustworthy world.

Introduction

In an era dominated by the relentless march of technology, the concept of privacy has taken center stage as a multifaceted issue that demands careful consideration. As the world has embraced the digital age, the evolution of communication platforms like WhatsApp has both enabled unprecedented connectivity and raised profound questions about the boundaries of personal privacy. This article delves into the complex landscape of privacy in the digital age within the context of WhatsApp's evolution, exploring crucial aspects such as encryption, data sharing, and the intricate balance of user control.

The Encryption Dilemma

One of the cornerstones of privacy in the digital age is encryption - a technology designed to protect the confidentiality of messages exchanged between users. WhatsApp, like many other messaging platforms, employs end-to-end encryption to safeguard conversations from prying eyes. This encryption mechanism ensures that only the intended recipient can decipher and access the content of the messages. While encryption provides a critical layer of security, it also raises concerns in the realm of law enforcement and national security.

Critics argue that encryption may inadvertently shield criminal activities, making it difficult for authorities to access vital information for investigation purposes. This conundrum pits the values of individual privacy against societal security interests. Striking the right balance between these competing priorities is a monumental challenge - one that requires careful consideration of legal frameworks and technological innovations.

Data Sharing

The digital landscape is awash with data, and WhatsApp is no exception. The platform collects a wealth of user data, ranging from personal information to usage patterns, in order to enhance user experience and enable targeted advertising. However, this data collection practice has ignited debates about the extent to which user information should be shared with third parties.

While WhatsApp has taken steps to minimize data sharing and provide users with a degree of control, concerns remain regarding the potential misuse of collected data. Instances of data breaches and unauthorized access underscore the fragility of personal information in the digital realm. The challenge lies in striking a delicate balance - enabling platforms to provide tailored services while safeguarding user data from unauthorized exploitation.

User Control

In the realm of digital privacy, the issue of user control is a paradoxical one. On one hand, users demand the autonomy to control the information they share and the visibility of their online presence. On the other, the complexity of modern communication platforms often places control mechanisms in the hands of service providers, leading to potential vulnerabilities.

WhatsApp's evolution has introduced features that attempt to empower users, such as customizable privacy settings and the ability to control who can see profile information. However, the intricacies of these settings can be daunting, leaving many users uncertain about the extent to which they can truly control their digital footprint. Striking the right balance between user empowerment and platform functionality necessitates intuitive interfaces and comprehensive user education.

The Role of Regulation

The digital age transcends geographical borders, presenting unique challenges for privacy regulation. WhatsApp's global user base means that its policies and practices must adhere to a patchwork of diverse legal frameworks. The European Union's General Data Protection Regulation (GDPR) and similar initiatives have set a precedent for data protection and privacy rights. However, achieving a harmonious global approach to digital privacy remains an ongoing endeavor.

The debate over whether governments should have the authority to regulate and monitor digital communication platforms has profound implications for individual rights and societal interests. Striking the right balance between local regulations and global connectivity requires international cooperation and the continuous adaptation of legal standards to the evolving technological landscape.

Educational Imperative

As the digital age continues to reshape how we communicate, an essential aspect of preserving privacy lies in promoting digital literacy and awareness. Many users may inadvertently share sensitive information or fall victim to phishing attacks due to a lack of understanding about the intricacies of online privacy.

Efforts to enhance digital literacy must encompass not only technical proficiency but also an understanding of the broader implications of digital footprints. By equipping users with the knowledge to make informed decisions about their online interactions, we can foster a more privacy-conscious and responsible digital society.

Conclusion

In the grand tapestry of the digital age, privacy stands as a thread that weaves through every interaction, every message, and every data point shared. WhatsApp's evolution serves as both a reflection of the opportunities brought forth by digital connectivity and a reminder of the challenges that come with it. Encryption, data sharing, user control, regulation, and education are the pillars that uphold this delicate balance between personal privacy and the demands of an interconnected world. As technology marches forward, the responsibility to navigate these complexities rests not only with platforms and regulators but with each individual who contributes to the digital fabric of our modern society.

Introduction

In an era dominated by digital communication, social interactions have undergone a remarkable transformation. Among the various digital platforms that have reshaped the landscape of human interaction, WhatsApp stands out as one of the most influential. This article delves into the intricate interplay between group dynamics and social identity within the realm of WhatsApp group chats, highlighting their role in shaping social behaviors – both positive and negative – and the evolving concept of digital responsibility.

The WhatsApp Revolution

The advent of smartphones and instant messaging apps brought about a revolution in the way people communicate. WhatsApp, with its ease of use and real-time messaging capabilities, quickly became a global phenomenon, connecting individuals across borders and time zones. Group chats emerged as a prominent feature, allowing users to interact within a collective space. However, beneath the convenience and connectivity lies a complex interplay of group dynamics and social identity that significantly influences the way individuals behave and perceive themselves in the digital realm.

Group Dynamics and Social Identity

Group dynamics refer to the interactions, relationships, and behaviors that manifest within a group setting. WhatsApp group chats provide a virtual platform for these dynamics to unfold, giving rise to both positive and negative outcomes. One of the key aspects of group dynamics is social identity – the way individuals define themselves based on the groups they belong to. Social identity is a crucial determinant of behavior, influencing how people perceive themselves and others, as well as their attitudes and actions within the group.

Formation of Social Identity in WhatsApp Groups

WhatsApp groups serve as catalysts for the formation and reinforcement of social identity. Group members develop a sense of belonging and identification with the group's purpose, values, and norms. This sense of belonging contributes to the development of a shared social identity, which, in turn, influences how individuals communicate and engage within the group chat.

Positive Social Behaviors

In many instances, WhatsApp group chats foster positive social behaviors. These groups create a space for individuals to share experiences, exchange ideas, and offer support. A sense of camaraderie emerges, often leading to the development of strong social bonds. Group members find solace in the collective identity, knowing they are part of a community that understands and empathizes with their challenges and triumphs.

Group chats centered around hobbies, interests, or causes exemplify this positive dynamic. Members bond over shared passions, engaging in meaningful discussions and collaborations. Whether it's a book club, a fitness group, or a volunteer organization, these groups encourage individuals to contribute positively to the collective identity while nurturing a sense of purpose and fulfillment.

Negative Social Behaviors

However, the same group dynamics that enable positive behaviors can also give rise to negative outcomes. WhatsApp group chats can inadvertently lead to polarization and the reinforcement of harmful biases. The anonymity provided by digital communication can embolden individuals to express extreme views or engage in toxic behaviors that they might refrain from in face-to-face interactions.

Social identity can amplify these negative behaviors. In-group favoritism and out-group hostility may arise, as members define themselves in opposition to perceived 'others.' This can result in echo chambers where dissenting opinions are silenced, hindering healthy debate and critical thinking.

Digital Responsibility in WhatsApp Group Chats

As the influence of WhatsApp group dynamics on social identity becomes increasingly evident, the concept of digital responsibility gains prominence. Digital responsibility entails a conscious and ethical approach to online interactions, recognizing the impact of one's words and actions on the broader digital community.

Fostering Positive Digital Spaces

To harness the positive potential of WhatsApp group chats, it is essential to foster inclusive and respectful digital spaces. Group administrators play a pivotal role in setting the tone for interactions, establishing guidelines that prioritize open dialogue and discourage toxic behaviors. Encouraging diverse perspectives and promoting empathy within the group can help counteract the negative aspects of social identity formation.

Mitigating Negative Behaviors

Addressing negative behaviors within WhatsApp group chats requires a multi-faceted approach. Group members should be educated about the consequences of polarized thinking and the dangers of unchecked anonymity. Emphasizing critical thinking and fact-based discussions can help break down echo chambers and promote a more responsible digital environment.

Conclusion

WhatsApp group chats have transformed the way people connect, communicate, and identify themselves in the digital age. The intricate interplay between group dynamics and social identity within these virtual spaces underscores the need for mindful digital responsibility. By recognizing the power of collective identity to shape behaviors, individuals can work towards fostering positive interactions, embracing diversity of thought, and mitigating the negative influences that can arise. As the WhatsApp evolution continues, the quest for responsible and ethical digital engagement remains paramount.

Introduction

In an era dominated by instant messaging platforms, WhatsApp has emerged as a global powerhouse, connecting individuals across continents and cultures in real time. The evolution of this application, however, comes hand in hand with the rise of a pressing issue: hate speech. The digital realm offers unprecedented opportunities for communication and engagement, but it also presents challenges in managing and curbing hate speech. This article delves into the complexities of combating hate speech on WhatsApp and explores potential solutions to foster a safer and more responsible digital environment.

The Pervasive Challenge of Hate Speech

Hate speech, a venomous rhetoric rooted in prejudice, discrimination, and hostility, has found an unfortunate haven on WhatsApp's expansive platform. This is a multifaceted issue, fueled by the anonymity, immediacy, and vast reach that the application offers. Hate speech can target various aspects such as race, religion, ethnicity, gender, sexual orientation, and more, causing real-world harm and perpetuating social divisions.

The anonymity factor, inherent in digital communication, emboldens individuals to express extreme views without the fear of immediate consequences. This creates an environment where hate speech can thrive, as perpetrators can shield their true identities behind screens. Additionally, the speed at which messages can be disseminated through

WhatsApp's forwarding feature amplifies the reach of hate speech, making it a challenge to control its spread.

Challenges in Combating Hate Speech on WhatsApp

1. Encryption and Privacy Concerns: WhatsApp's end-to-end encryption, while crucial for protecting user privacy, also poses a challenge in monitoring and moderating hate speech. Encryption ensures that only the sender and receiver can read the content of messages, making it difficult for authorities and platforms to identify and intervene in cases of hate speech.

2. Language and Context: Hate speech can often be nuanced and context-dependent, making it difficult for automated systems to accurately identify and moderate such content. The application's diverse user base and the multitude of languages further complicate the task of effective monitoring.

3. Balancing Freedom of Expression: The fine line between freedom of expression and hate speech is a contentious issue. Striking a balance between curtailing hate speech and upholding the principles of free speech is a delicate task, often leading to debates about censorship and overreach.

Solutions to Cultivate a Safer Digital Environment

1. Algorithmic Monitoring and Moderation: WhatsApp can invest in advanced algorithms that employ natural language processing (NLP) to detect hate speech. While not a foolproof solution, these algorithms can significantly assist in identifying and flagging potentially harmful content. However, this approach should be complemented by human review, as AI algorithms can sometimes misinterpret context.

2. User Reporting and Community Moderation: Empowering users to report hate speech and offensive content is an effective way to crowdsource moderation efforts. WhatsApp could implement a streamlined reporting system, enabling users to flag problematic messages. Community moderation, where trusted users assist in reviewing reported content, can also enhance the efficiency of content moderation.

3. Education and Awareness: Promoting digital responsibility and imparting awareness about the consequences of hate speech is vital. WhatsApp can collaborate with NGOs, educational institutions, and governments to develop campaigns that educate users about the impact of hate speech and the importance of respectful communication.

4. Contextual Analysis: Developing AI systems that can understand the context of messages is crucial. AI tools that consider linguistic nuances, cultural references, and historical context can better differentiate between hate speech and legitimate discussions, reducing the risk of false positives.

5. Encouraging Positive Engagement: WhatsApp can implement features that encourage positive interactions, such as highlighting constructive discussions and rewarding users who contribute positively to the platform. This can shift the focus away from negativity and foster a more inclusive online community.

6. Transparency and Accountability: WhatsApp can enhance transparency by regularly sharing information about its content moderation efforts, including the number of reported cases, actions taken, and updates on policy

changes. This can instill confidence in users that the platform is actively combating hate speech.

7. Collaboration with Law Enforcement: While respecting user privacy, WhatsApp can collaborate with law enforcement agencies to address serious instances of hate speech that might incite violence or pose imminent threats. Striking the right balance between privacy and safety is crucial in such collaborations.

Conclusion

WhatsApp's evolution has revolutionized communication, but it has also exposed the vulnerabilities of digital discourse, notably hate speech. As technology advances, the responsibility to create a safer digital environment lies not only with platforms like WhatsApp but also with its users. Addressing hate speech requires a multi-pronged approach that combines technological innovation, education, collaboration, and fostering a sense of responsibility among users.

By leveraging the power of AI, investing in user education, and promoting positive engagement, WhatsApp can pave the way for a future where hate speech is marginalized and responsible digital communication flourishes. As users of this transformative platform, it is our collective duty to participate actively in creating a virtual world that mirrors the values of respect, empathy, and inclusivity that we uphold in our physical lives.

Introduction

In an age defined by rapid technological advancements and widespread digital connectivity, messaging applications have emerged as the cornerstone of modern communication. Among these, WhatsApp has undoubtedly been a trailblazer, evolving from a simple text messaging platform to a multifaceted communication tool. However, the evolution of WhatsApp hasn't been without its share of challenges, particularly concerning security vulnerabilities. This article delves into the realm of WhatsApp's security journey, exploring the technical vulnerabilities it has encountered and the measures taken to bolster user security. By understanding these dynamics, we can navigate the intricate landscape of digital responsibility and ensure that our interactions remain secure in this ever-changing digital ecosystem.

The Technological Landscape of WhatsApp Evolution

In its inception, WhatsApp offered a revolutionary approach to instant messaging, endearing itself to users worldwide with its user-friendly interface and cross-platform compatibility. As it evolved, the application integrated voice and video calling, media sharing, and encryption technologies, elevating its functionality and appeal. However, this evolution wasn't immune to the evolving landscape of cybersecurity.

Unveiling Vulnerabilities

1. Privacy Breaches and Data Leaks

WhatsApp, like many other digital platforms, encountered its fair share of privacy breaches and data leaks. In 2014, a security flaw was discovered that allowed hackers to intercept and manipulate messages. There was an incident involving Jeff Bezos, the CEO of Amazon, where his personal phone was allegedly hacked in 2018. The incident reportedly involved the hacking of his phone through a WhatsApp message that contained malware. The incident led to the unauthorized access of Bezos's private data, including text messages and photos. The incident involving the breach of Jeff Bezos' phone underscored the potential vulnerabilities associated with WhatsApp, emphasizing the need for continual vigilance.

2. Pegasus Spyware: A Grim Intrusion

The revelation of the Pegasus spyware incident in 2021 sent shockwaves through the tech community. Exploiting a vulnerability in the WhatsApp calling feature, this sophisticated spyware compromised the devices of numerous individuals, highlighting the implications of security lapses on a global scale.

3. Account Takeovers and Phishing Attacks

WhatsApp has also been a target for cybercriminals seeking to execute phishing attacks and hijack user accounts. These attacks leverage social engineering tactics, preying on users' trust and lack of awareness, thereby emphasizing the crucial role of user education in enhancing overall security.

Fortifying Security Measures

1. End-to-End Encryption

Recognizing the need for heightened security, WhatsApp implemented end-to-end encryption, ensuring that only the sender and recipient can access the content of a message. This cryptographic protocol mitigates the risk of unauthorized access and eavesdropping, bolstering user privacy.

2. Two-Step Verification

To combat unauthorized access and account takeovers, WhatsApp introduced two-step verification. This feature requires users to enter a unique PIN in addition to their phone number when setting up their account, adding an extra layer of security.

3. Regular Software Updates

WhatsApp's security team works diligently to identify and address vulnerabilities promptly. Regular software updates are crucial in patching known security flaws and strengthening the application's overall resilience to cyber threats.

4. Collaboration with Security Researchers

WhatsApp actively engages with the global cybersecurity community by partnering with independent researchers and organizations to identify and rectify security vulnerabilities. This collaborative approach fosters a collective commitment to safeguarding user security.

Navigating Digital Responsibility

1. User Education and Awareness

Empowering users with knowledge about potential security risks and safe digital practices is paramount. Educating users about identifying phishing attempts, practicing caution with shared media, and understanding the implications of granting application permissions are essential steps in fostering digital responsibility.

2. Privacy Settings and Controls

WhatsApp equips users with a range of privacy settings and controls that enable them to tailor their security preferences. From controlling who can view their profile picture to managing who can add them to groups, these features empower users to curate their digital interactions.

3. Reporting Suspicious Activity

Users play a pivotal role in maintaining the security of the platform by promptly reporting suspicious activities and potential security breaches. This collaborative effort ensures that WhatsApp's security team can swiftly address emerging threats.

The Road Ahead

As WhatsApp continues to evolve and adapt to the dynamic digital landscape, the importance of security remains paramount. The challenges faced along its journey underscore the necessity for constant vigilance and innovation. By harnessing cutting-edge technologies, collaborating with cybersecurity experts, and fostering user awareness, WhatsApp strives to stay ahead of potential vulnerabilities and uphold its commitment to user security.

Conclusion

WhatsApp's evolution from a fledgling messaging application to a global communication giant has been marked by remarkable strides and undeniable challenges. Navigating the complex terrain of security vulnerabilities, the platform has demonstrated its commitment to enhancing user security through encryption, regular updates, and collaborative efforts. Nevertheless, the onus of digital responsibility falls not only on the developers but also on the users themselves. By understanding the landscape of potential threats, adopting security best practices, and engaging in a collective effort to maintain a secure digital environment, users can contribute to a safer and more responsible digital future. As WhatsApp's journey continues, the pursuit of security and the preservation of digital responsibility remain essential pillars in its evolution.

Chapter 11. Digital Literacy and Critical Thinking

Introduction

In the rapidly evolving digital landscape, WhatsApp has emerged as a ubiquitous platform that transcends geographical boundaries, connecting individuals across the globe in real-time communication. As the digital era continues to unfold, it brings with it both unprecedented opportunities and formidable challenges. Central among these challenges is the need for individuals to develop robust digital literacy skills and cultivate critical thinking abilities. In the context of "WhatsApp Evolution and Digital Responsibility," the symbiotic relationship between digital literacy and critical thinking takes center stage, equipping users to navigate the complexities of information consumption and dissemination responsibly and effectively.

The WhatsApp Evolution

WhatsApp, since its inception, has undergone a remarkable evolution, transforming from a simple text messaging app to a multifaceted communication ecosystem. From text to voice calls, video calls, group chats, and the integration of multimedia, the platform has woven itself into the fabric of our daily lives. This evolution, while enhancing connectivity, has also ushered in a deluge of information that demands discernment and evaluation. As the platform continues to adapt and introduce new features, users must rise to the occasion by honing their digital literacy skills and embracing critical thinking.

Unraveling Digital Literacy

Digital literacy encompasses a spectrum of skills that empower individuals to engage with, comprehend, and navigate the digital landscape adeptly. It is more than the mere ability to use technological tools; it entails the capacity to critically assess, analyze, and interpret the information encountered. In the context of WhatsApp, digital literacy translates to the skillset required to evaluate the authenticity, credibility, and relevance of the messages and media flooding our screens.

The process of digital literacy involves deciphering the intentions behind forwarded messages, understanding the nuances of multimedia content, and discerning the credibility of sources. Users must possess the ability to fact-check, distinguish between credible and unreliable information, and recognize the potential pitfalls of misinformation and disinformation.

Misinformation refers to false or inaccurate information that is spread without the intent to deceive. It can occur due to misunderstandings, mistakes, or the sharing of outdated or incorrect data, often without malicious intent. Disinformation, on the other hand, refers to deliberately false or misleading information that is spread with the intention to deceive, manipulate opinions, or achieve some other ulterior motive. It is often used as a tool for propaganda, influencing public perception, or advancing a particular agenda. Both misinformation and disinformation can have significant consequences, including shaping public opinion, influencing decision-making, and contributing to the spread of false beliefs or harmful actions.

Digital literacy is the compass that enables individuals to traverse the vast sea of information on WhatsApp, ensuring that they are not led astray by the currents of misinformation.

The Crucial Role of Critical Thinking

Critical thinking, often regarded as the pinnacle of cognitive evolution, is the cornerstone of responsible and informed engagement with digital content. It entails the active and deliberate analysis of information, questioning assumptions, and evaluating evidence before arriving at conclusions. In the context of WhatsApp, critical thinking serves as the mental armament that guards against the infiltration of misleading or harmful content.

Critical thinking prompts users to consider the source of a message, the potential biases at play, and the credibility of the claims being made. It encourages skepticism without dismissing information outright, fostering a balanced approach that hinges on evidence-based evaluation. By fostering critical thinking, users are empowered to sift through the virtual influx of information, separating the wheat from the chaff and making informed decisions.

Digital Responsibility

The synergy between digital literacy and critical thinking forms the bedrock of digital responsibility. To fully embrace the evolution of WhatsApp and its implications, users must bridge the gap between acquiring digital literacy skills and applying critical thinking. Digital responsibility encompasses both understanding the technicalities of the platform and wielding critical thinking as a shield against the potential pitfalls of misinformation.

Being digitally responsible on WhatsApp entails considering the ripple effects of sharing information. It involves refraining from forwarding unverified claims, sensationalized news, or clickbait without first evaluating their veracity. It is the conscious effort to engage in constructive dialogues, engage in fact-checking, and contribute to the dissemination of accurate information. Digital responsibility is the moral compass that guides users to treat information with the same caution and thoughtfulness they would in offline interactions.

Educational Imperative

The evolution of WhatsApp demands an educational imperative that prioritizes the cultivation of digital literacy and critical thinking from an early age. Educational institutions and policymakers have a vital role to play in integrating these skills into curricula, fostering a generation of digital citizens equipped to navigate the evolving landscape responsibly.

Educators can introduce lessons that teach students how to verify sources, critically assess information, and engage in respectful online discourse. By emphasizing the importance of cross-referencing information and weighing different perspectives, educators can empower students to become discerning consumers and contributors in the digital realm.

Conclusion

In the dynamic realm of WhatsApp evolution, the synergy between digital literacy and critical thinking serves as the lodestar guiding individuals through the tumultuous seas of information. The skills to decipher, question, and analyze information are paramount in the age of digital communication. As users, we must embrace the responsibility that comes with wielding the power of connectivity and contribute to a digital landscape marked by integrity, accuracy, and thoughtful engagement. Just as WhatsApp continues to evolve, so must our approach to information consumption and dissemination, grounded in the twin pillars of digital literacy and critical thinking. By doing so, we embark on a journey towards a more informed, responsible, and empowered digital future.

Chapter 12. Cultivating Healthy Online Habits

Introduction

In an age dominated by technology and connectivity, the evolution of communication platforms has transformed the way we interact with the world around us. Among these platforms, WhatsApp has emerged as a ubiquitous tool, bridging distances and connecting people across the globe. As the digital landscape continues to evolve, so do the responsibilities that come with it. The need for cultivating healthy online habits has never been more crucial, especially when it comes to managing our time spent on WhatsApp and maintaining a harmonious balance between our online and offline lives.

Understanding the Digital Transformation

The advent of WhatsApp revolutionized communication, transcending geographical boundaries and allowing instantaneous exchanges of messages, images, and videos. Its evolution has been marked by constant updates, offering new features and functionalities that enhance the user experience. However, with these advancements comes the challenge of responsible usage.

Recognizing the Importance of Balance

As the allure of WhatsApp draws us into its captivating realm, it becomes imperative to strike a balance between our virtual interactions and the tangible world. Failing to do so can lead to digital burnout, strained relationships, and a diminished sense of well-being. Here are strategies to help you cultivate healthy online habits and ensure that the evolution of WhatsApp is met with digital responsibility.

1. Set Intentional Boundaries

The boundary between online and offline life can often blur, leading to an unhealthy obsession with constant connectivity. Establish specific timeframes for engaging with WhatsApp. Designate periods for work-related conversations, personal interactions, and moments of complete detachment. By creating intentional boundaries, you regain control over your time and reduce the risk of being consumed by the digital realm.

2. Practice Mindful Engagement

Mindfulness is a powerful tool that can reshape the way we interact with technology. When using WhatsApp, focus on the present moment. Avoid mindless scrolling and instead, engage with purpose. Be fully present during conversations, absorbing the content and context of messages. This not only enhances the quality of your interactions but also prevents you from becoming a passive recipient of digital information.

3. Embrace the Art of Digital Detox

Just as our bodies require rest to rejuvenate, our digital selves also need periodic detoxification. Dedicate regular intervals to disconnect from WhatsApp and other digital platforms. Utilize this time to engage in hobbies, outdoor activities, or face-to-face interactions. A digital detox not only reduces screen time but also allows you to rediscover the joys of offline life.

4. Curate Your Digital Circle

The evolution of WhatsApp has led to expansive networks, connecting us with acquaintances, colleagues, and friends of friends. However, a larger network doesn't necessarily equate to more meaningful connections. Regularly assess your contacts and groups. Weed out those that contribute to negative experiences or do not align with your interests and values. Cultivate a digital circle that enriches your online interactions.

5. Prioritize Real-Time Connections

While WhatsApp facilitates instant messaging, it should not replace the depth of face-to-face interactions. Allocate time for in-person meetings with friends, family, and colleagues. These real-time connections offer emotional nuances and non-verbal cues that are often lost in digital exchanges. Balancing virtual conversations with personal encounters fosters a well-rounded social life.

6. Harness the Power of Digital Tools

Paradoxically, technology can also aid in managing technology itself. Utilize the features within WhatsApp that allow you to control notifications and mute conversations during specific hours. Explore time management apps that track your screen time and provide insights into your digital habits. Leveraging digital tools empowers you to make informed decisions about your online engagement.

7. Cultivate Offline Hobbies

To strike a harmonious balance between your online and offline worlds, invest time in cultivating offline hobbies and interests. Engaging in creative pursuits, physical activities, or simply reading a book can provide a sense of fulfillment that transcends the virtual realm. Diversifying your interests not only enriches your life but also reduces dependency on constant online engagement.

8. Educate and Lead by Example

As the evolution of WhatsApp continues, it is crucial to impart the principles of digital responsibility to younger generations. Educate children and teenagers about the importance of time management, mindful engagement, and the value of real-world connections. Lead by example, demonstrating how to navigate the digital landscape while preserving one's well-being.

Conclusion

The evolution of WhatsApp reflects the dynamic nature of technology and its profound impact on our lives. As we harness the capabilities of this platform, let us also recognize the responsibility that comes with it. Cultivating healthy online habits is not just a personal endeavor but a collective commitment to nurturing a digital ecosystem that fosters well-being, meaningful connections, and a harmonious balance between our virtual and offline lives. By setting intentional boundaries, practicing mindful engagement, and embracing the art of digital detox, we can navigate the evolving landscape of WhatsApp with wisdom and digital responsibility.

Introduction

In today's digitally interconnected world, social media platforms play a significant role in shaping communities and fostering interactions among individuals from diverse backgrounds. WhatsApp, a widely used messaging application, has evolved to become more than just a tool for communication; it has become a platform for building inclusive communities. In this article, we delve into the importance of inclusive communities, explore the evolution of WhatsApp as a community-building tool, and discuss how its features can be harnessed for positive community development while upholding digital responsibility.

Understanding Inclusive Communities

Inclusive communities are social environments that embrace and value diversity, where individuals from various backgrounds, identities, abilities, and perspectives feel welcomed, respected, and empowered. These communities actively promote equal opportunities, equitable treatment, and meaningful participation for all members, regardless of their differences, and work to eliminate barriers that may lead to exclusion or discrimination. Inclusive communities strive to foster a sense of belonging, collaboration, and mutual understanding among their members, ultimately creating a more just and harmonious society.

Inclusive communities are the heart of a harmonious and diverse society. They provide individuals with a sense of belonging, encourage open dialogue, and facilitate the exchange of ideas, experiences, and perspectives. These communities transcend geographical boundaries, enabling people to connect and collaborate across cultures, languages, and backgrounds. Inclusivity in digital communities is crucial as it mirrors the inclusive values we aspire to in our physical world.

WhatsApp's Evolution as a Community-Building Tool

From its inception as a simple messaging app to its current state as a multifaceted communication platform, WhatsApp has undergone a remarkable evolution. Originally designed for one-on-one communication, WhatsApp has now expanded its features to accommodate group chats, voice and video calls, status updates, and document sharing. This evolution has paved the way for diverse groups of people to come together, share their stories, and forge meaningful connections.

Leveraging WhatsApp's Features for Positive Community Development

1. Group Chats

Group chats are at the core of WhatsApp's community-building potential. They allow like-minded individuals to gather, share information, and discuss topics of interest. To build inclusive communities, group admins should establish clear guidelines that promote respectful discourse and discourage discriminatory behavior. By facilitating healthy conversations, group admins can foster a sense of belonging and encourage members to learn from each other's unique experiences.

2. Voice and Video Calls

WhatsApp's voice and video call features transcend textual communication, enabling individuals to have real-time conversations regardless of their location. This feature can be harnessed to bridge cultural gaps and enhance cross-cultural understanding. Communities can organize virtual events, workshops, or language exchange sessions, promoting interaction and empathy among members with diverse linguistic and cultural backgrounds.

3. Status Updates

Status updates allow users to share their thoughts, experiences, and feelings through multimedia content. Communities can leverage this feature to showcase personal narratives and celebrate diverse perspectives. By encouraging members to share their stories, communities can create an environment where individuals feel valued and understood, contributing to a sense of inclusivity.

4. Document Sharing

The ability to share documents on WhatsApp facilitates knowledge exchange within communities. This feature can be used to distribute educational materials, research findings, or relevant articles. Inclusive communities can organize virtual book clubs, where members from different walks of life come together to discuss literature and exchange insights, fostering intellectual growth and understanding.

Digital Responsibility

While WhatsApp's features offer great potential for building inclusive communities, it is essential to uphold digital responsibility to ensure a safe and respectful environment.

1. Moderation and Guidelines

Group administrators should establish clear guidelines that outline acceptable behavior and prohibit hate speech, discrimination, and harassment. Active moderation ensures that the community remains a welcoming space for all members.

2. Educational Initiatives

Promote digital literacy within the community, educating members about responsible online behavior, fact-checking, and respectful communication. By equipping members with these skills, the community becomes a more informed and compassionate space.

3. Reporting and Blocking

WhatsApp's reporting and blocking features empower users to take action against inappropriate behavior. Encourage community members to report instances of abuse or misconduct, ensuring that harmful behavior is addressed promptly.

4. Privacy Considerations

Respecting members' privacy is crucial for building trust within the community. Encourage members to be mindful of the personal information they share and provide guidance on adjusting privacy settings to maintain a sense of security.

Conclusion

WhatsApp's evolution from a simple messaging app to a versatile communication platform has opened doors to a new era of community building. By harnessing its features thoughtfully and responsibly, we can create inclusive communities that celebrate diversity, encourage meaningful interactions, and promote empathy across borders. In a world where digital connections are becoming increasingly influential, the role of platforms like WhatsApp in shaping inclusive communities is more vital than ever. Let us embrace this opportunity to build communities that reflect the richness and beauty of our global society while upholding the values of respect, understanding, and digital responsibility.

Introduction

In the rapidly evolving digital landscape, WhatsApp has emerged as one of the most widely used messaging platforms, transforming how we communicate and share information. With this evolution comes a pressing need for digital responsibility, particularly in the realm of information dissemination. The sheer speed and ease of sharing messages on WhatsApp make it imperative to prioritize accuracy and fact-checking to prevent the spread of misinformation. This article delves into the crucial aspect of promoting fact-checking and accuracy within the context of WhatsApp's evolution, offering guidance on verifying information before sharing and debunking common myths.

The Evolution of WhatsApp and the Challenge of Digital Responsibility

WhatsApp has undergone a remarkable transformation since its inception, evolving from a simple text messaging platform to a multimedia-rich communication tool. This evolution has brought both immense convenience and significant challenges. While the platform's features facilitate seamless sharing of information, they also make it susceptible to the rapid dissemination of misinformation and falsehoods. This underscores the need for users to exercise digital responsibility by fact-checking and verifying information before hitting the 'forward' button.

The Role of Fact-Checking in the Era of Instant Communication

In the age of instant communication, the traditional gatekeepers of information, such as news outlets and publishers, have been bypassed. This has led to a democratization of information sharing, but it has also opened the floodgates for unverified and false content to spread unchecked. Fact-checking has emerged as a vital tool to counteract this phenomenon. The process of fact-checking involves critically assessing the accuracy of claims, verifying sources, and cross-referencing information before sharing it with a wider audience. WhatsApp users must understand that they, too, bear a responsibility to fact-check the content they share, acting as micro-gatekeepers to curb the dissemination of misinformation.

Guidelines for Verifying Information Before Sharing

1. Source Evaluation: Before sharing any information, users should assess the credibility of the source. Reputable news organizations, official government websites, and established research institutions are generally reliable sources. Suspicious or obscure websites lacking proper attribution and citations should be approached with skepticism.

2. Cross-Verification: Cross-referencing information with multiple sources can help ensure its accuracy. If a claim or news story is only reported by one source, it is advisable to wait for confirmation from other trusted outlets before sharing.

3. Check for Citations: Articles or posts that lack proper citations or references should be treated cautiously.

Legitimate information is typically supported by a trail of credible sources.

4. Expert Consensus: In cases involving scientific or technical information, it is wise to consult experts or authoritative figures in the relevant field. Their insights can help validate or debunk claims.

Debunking Common Myths

1. Health and Medical Misinformation: WhatsApp has been a breeding ground for health-related myths and misinformation, especially during global health crises. Users should critically evaluate claims related to cures, treatments, and preventive measures by consulting reputable health organizations like the World Health Organization (WHO) or the Centers for Disease Control and Prevention (CDC).

2. Political and Social Issues: Misinformation often proliferates around political events and social issues. Users must be cautious of sensational claims or incendiary content that lacks verifiable evidence. Cross-referencing statements made by politicians or public figures with trusted news sources can help determine their accuracy.

3. Historical Claims: WhatsApp's reach has enabled the spread of historical inaccuracies. Users should approach forwarded messages about historical events with skepticism and verify claims through reliable historical records, academic research, or expert opinions.

4. Chain Messages and Urban Legends: WhatsApp is notorious for circulating chain messages and urban legends. Users should critically assess the authenticity of such messages before forwarding them. Fact-checking websites

and online debunking resources can be valuable tools in dispelling these myths.

Promoting Digital Literacy and Education

Promoting fact-checking and accuracy on WhatsApp goes hand in hand with fostering digital literacy and education. Users should be empowered with the skills to critically evaluate information, discern credible sources, and differentiate between opinion and fact. Educators, community leaders, and technology companies can collaborate to develop educational initiatives that equip individuals with the tools they need to navigate the digital landscape responsibly.

Conclusion

WhatsApp's evolution has revolutionized communication, enabling the sharing of information on an unprecedented scale. However, this power comes with great responsibility. Users must recognize their role in curbing the spread of misinformation by prioritizing fact-checking and accuracy. By following guidelines for verifying information and debunking common myths, individuals can contribute to a more responsible and informed digital environment. As we continue to witness the evolution of WhatsApp and other digital platforms, our commitment to truth and accuracy remains a cornerstone of a healthier, more connected world.

Introduction

In today's rapidly evolving digital landscape, technological trends and innovations play a pivotal role in shaping the trajectory of various platforms and applications. One such platform that has become an integral part of our lives is WhatsApp. As we delve into the evolution of WhatsApp and its integration into emerging technologies, it becomes evident that its journey is closely intertwined with the principles of digital responsibility.

The Evolution of WhatsApp

WhatsApp, founded in 2009, started as a simple instant messaging application, allowing users to send text messages over the internet. However, its potential for transforming communication soon became apparent. The introduction of multimedia sharing, voice messages, and group chats revolutionized how people connected and interacted across distances. Over the years, video calling, voice calling, and end-to-end encryption bolstered its security and capabilities, making it a global communication giant.

Artificial Intelligence and Chatbots

The integration of artificial intelligence (AI) and chatbots has propelled WhatsApp into the realm of personalized and efficient communication. AI algorithms now power features such as predictive text, smart replies, and contextual suggestions. Chatbots have made customer interactions seamless, providing instant responses and streamlining inquiries. This convergence of AI and messaging not only enhances user experience but also sets the stage for AI-driven virtual assistants within the platform.

Internet of Things (IoT) Integration

Internet of Things (IoT) refers to the network of interconnected devices that can collect, exchange, and process data through the internet. As the Internet of Things (IoT) continues to expand its reach, WhatsApp's integration with IoT devices opens up a new dimension of connectivity. Smart home systems, wearable devices, and other IoT gadgets can now be controlled and monitored through WhatsApp. This convergence enables users to manage their surroundings remotely, whether it's adjusting home temperature, receiving security alerts, or tracking health metrics. Such integration underscores WhatsApp's role as a central hub for diverse digital interactions.

Blockchain and Enhanced Security

Blockchain enhances security by providing a tamper-proof and transparent record of transactions, making it difficult to alter or manipulate data, and enabling secure peer-to-peer transactions without the need for intermediaries. Blockchain technology is at the forefront of enhancing security and digital trust. WhatsApp's potential adoption of blockchain could lead to improved data privacy, secure identity verification, and tamper-proof messaging. Decentralized storage and authentication mechanisms would empower users to have greater control over their data, reducing the risks associated with centralized data storage. This shift aligns with the principles of digital responsibility by putting data ownership back into the hands of users.

Augmented Reality (AR) and Virtual Reality (VR)

Augmented Reality (AR) overlays digital information or virtual objects onto the real-world environment, enhancing the user's perception, while Virtual Reality (VR) immerses users in a completely simulated digital environment, often through the use of headsets and controllers. The integration of augmented reality (AR) and virtual reality (VR) technologies into WhatsApp could revolutionize how we communicate. Imagine sharing immersive experiences with friends and family, attending virtual meetings, or collaborating on projects through AR and VR interfaces. WhatsApp's potential as a platform for such interactions could redefine the boundaries of digital communication, fostering deeper connections in virtual spaces.

Sustainable Technology and Green Communication

Sustainable technology focuses on creating environmentally friendly solutions, while green communication involves using eco-friendly practices and technologies to minimize environmental impact in the field of communication and information exchange. In an era of heightened environmental consciousness, the concept of sustainable technology is gaining traction. WhatsApp, as a data-intensive platform, has the opportunity to adopt eco-friendly practices. This could involve optimizing data transmission, reducing energy consumption, and promoting digital well-being among users. By incorporating sustainable technology principles, WhatsApp can contribute to a greener digital ecosystem while promoting responsible digital habits.

Ethical AI and Combating Misinformation

Ethical AI involves developing artificial intelligence systems that adhere to moral and societal principles, while combating misinformation entails efforts to prevent the spread of false or misleading information through various means, including AI-driven tools and fact-checking processes. The proliferation of misinformation and fake news is a pressing concern in the digital age. WhatsApp's integration with ethical AI solutions could serve as a powerful tool against the spread of false information. AI algorithms could analyze message content, flag potential misinformation, and provide users with contextual information to make informed judgments. This approach aligns with the concept of digital responsibility, empowering users to be critical consumers of information.

Quantum Computing and Next-Level Encryption

Quantum computing explores advanced computational principles using quantum bits (qubits), potentially revolutionizing encryption by enabling powerful algorithms that could break current cryptographic methods, prompting the need for next-level encryption techniques resistant to quantum attacks. The advent of quantum computing presents both opportunities and challenges for encryption. WhatsApp's exploration of quantum-resistant encryption could pave the way for unbreakable security measures, ensuring that user data remains confidential even in the face of quantum threats. This proactive approach to encryption aligns with digital responsibility, safeguarding user privacy in an increasingly complex digital landscape.

Inclusive Technology and Accessibility

Inclusive technology focuses on designing and developing tools, products, and services that are accessible and usable by people of diverse abilities, ensuring equitable participation and removing barriers to information, communication, and interaction. The future of WhatsApp lies in its commitment to inclusive technology. Features catering to individuals with disabilities, such as improved voice recognition, text-to-speech capabilities, and adaptive interfaces, can enhance the accessibility of the platform. By ensuring that everyone can seamlessly communicate and engage, WhatsApp demonstrates its dedication to digital responsibility and inclusivity.

Conclusion

As we contemplate the potential future developments of WhatsApp and its integration into emerging technologies, the concept of digital responsibility emerges as a guiding principle. WhatsApp's evolution from a simple messaging app to a multifaceted communication hub reflects the transformative power of technological innovation. Embracing trends like AI, IoT, blockchain, AR, and sustainable technology, WhatsApp can shape a future where connectivity, security, and inclusivity converge harmoniously.

In the rapidly evolving digital landscape, the responsibility lies not only with technology developers but also with users. Adhering to ethical practices, promoting digital literacy, and fostering a culture of critical thinking are vital components of navigating the digital realm responsibly. As WhatsApp continues its journey, it has the potential to not only redefine communication but also set new standards for digital responsibility, ensuring a future where technology serves as a force for positive change.

Introduction

In an era of rapid technological advancements, few platforms have reshaped communication and connectivity as profoundly as WhatsApp. This messaging application, born in 2009, has revolutionized the way individuals, communities, and businesses interact, transcending geographical boundaries and time zones. However, as WhatsApp and similar digital platforms have evolved, the need for robust regulation and effective governance mechanisms has become increasingly evident. This article delves into the multifaceted landscape of regulation and governance within the context of WhatsApp's evolution, exploring the roles of both governments and tech companies in addressing the challenges that have emerged.

The WhatsApp Revolution

WhatsApp's journey began as a simple messaging app, allowing users to send text messages over the internet rather than traditional SMS. Its initial appeal lay in its user-friendly interface, cost-effectiveness, and end-to-end encryption. As the app gained traction, it introduced features like voice calls, video calls, group chats, and multimedia sharing, transforming it into a comprehensive communication ecosystem.

The evolution of WhatsApp brought both opportunities and challenges. On one hand, it empowered businesses to engage with customers, facilitated family connections across borders, and enabled swift dissemination of information during crises. On the other hand, concerns emerged regarding misinformation, privacy breaches, cyberbullying, and the platform's potential misuse for criminal activities.

Regulation

Governments worldwide have grappled with the need to regulate digital platforms like WhatsApp. Balancing the imperative to foster innovation with the responsibility to protect users and society at large is a delicate task. Regulation in this context encompasses a range of measures, including legal frameworks, policies, and guidelines aimed at ensuring ethical conduct, user safety, and accountability.

1. Privacy and Data Protection: With the growing concern over data privacy, governments have moved to enact legislation such as the General Data Protection Regulation (GDPR) in the European Union and the California Consumer Privacy Act (CCPA) in the United States. These laws empower users with greater control over their personal data and require companies to be transparent about data usage. WhatsApp, as a platform handling vast amounts of user data, must adhere to these regulations to maintain trust and compliance.

2. Disinformation and Misinformation: The unchecked spread of false information on platforms like WhatsApp has raised alarm bells globally. Governments have sought to address this by pressuring tech companies to implement measures that curb misinformation, such as labeling forwarded messages, limiting message forwarding, and collaborating with fact-checking organizations. Striking a balance between curbing misinformation and preserving freedom of expression remains a challenge.

3. Encryption and Law Enforcement: The end-to-end encryption that ensures the privacy of WhatsApp conversations has also sparked debates over its impact on law enforcement efforts. Governments argue that such encryption can impede investigations into criminal activities. The tension between safeguarding user privacy and aiding law enforcement in legitimate cases requires careful consideration and possibly collaborative solutions.

Tech Companies

While governments play a vital role in regulating digital platforms, tech companies like WhatsApp bear significant responsibility in ensuring ethical use and user safety. These companies possess the technical expertise, resources, and influence to shape user experiences and mitigate potential risks.

1. Product Design and User Experience: Tech companies wield immense influence over how users engage with their platforms. Design choices, such as default settings and user interface elements, can impact privacy and security. Companies like WhatsApp must prioritize user education, making privacy features easily accessible and comprehensible.

2. Algorithmic Transparency: Algorithms that power content recommendations and moderation play a pivotal role in shaping user interactions. Greater transparency in how these algorithms function can help users understand why they see certain content and mitigate filter bubbles and echo chambers.

3. Collaborative Efforts: Tech companies can collaborate with governments, civil society organizations, and academia to address digital responsibility challenges

collectively. Partnerships can foster the development of innovative solutions to combat misinformation, cyberbullying, and other issues that transcend geographic boundaries.

The Need for Synergy

The dynamic landscape of digital communication calls for a synergy between governments and tech companies, where collaborative efforts are central to ensuring responsible platform evolution. This partnership can manifest in various ways:

1. Consultative Frameworks: Governments and tech companies can establish consultative frameworks that facilitate open dialogues on regulatory issues. Regular discussions can lead to informed policy decisions that balance innovation and user protection.

2. Data Sharing for Public Good: Collaborative data-sharing initiatives, where anonymized and aggregated data is shared with researchers and public health agencies, can help combat challenges like disease outbreaks and disinformation campaigns.

3. Research and Innovation Grants: Governments can provide grants and funding for research and innovation projects aimed at addressing digital responsibility concerns. This support can foster the development of tools and technologies that enhance user safety and ethical use.

Looking Ahead

As WhatsApp continues to evolve, its impact on society, communication, and commerce will only intensify. The role of regulation and governance in shaping this evolution is pivotal. Governments and tech companies must rise to the occasion, collaboratively crafting a landscape that prioritizes user safety, privacy, and responsible digital interactions.

Conclusion

The journey of WhatsApp from a simple messaging app to a global communication powerhouse reflects the transformative potential of technology. However, this potential comes with a responsibility to ensure that this transformation is guided by ethical principles and regulatory frameworks. Governments and tech companies are integral to this endeavor, each playing a unique role in steering WhatsApp's evolution and nurturing a digital realm that empowers, connects, and safeguards its users.

Introduction

The rapid evolution of communication technologies has transformed the way we connect and share information. Among the pioneers in this digital revolution is WhatsApp, a messaging application that has redefined communication on a global scale. However, as technology advances, so does the need for responsible and ethical design to ensure that these platforms enhance our lives without compromising our well-being and privacy. This article explores the concept of ethical design and how a user-centric approach can address some of the drawbacks associated with WhatsApp.

Understanding Ethical Design

Ethical design refers to the conscious and deliberate effort to create products, services, and experiences that prioritize the well-being of users, society, and the environment. In the context of digital platforms like WhatsApp, ethical design involves making intentional choices that promote user safety, privacy, and overall satisfaction. It shifts the focus from solely maximizing profits to creating products that align with users' values and respect their rights. Ethical design encompasses several key principles.

1. User Privacy and Data Security

One of the primary concerns in the digital age is the protection of user data. Ethical design dictates that platforms like WhatsApp should implement robust encryption and security measures to safeguard users' personal information from unauthorized access and breaches.

2. Transparency and Accountability

Ethical design encourages platforms to be transparent about their data collection and usage practices. Users should be informed about how their data is being utilized and have the ability to control their preferences.

3. Inclusivity and Accessibility

A user-centric approach means designing products that cater to a diverse range of users, including those with disabilities. WhatsApp, as a global platform, should ensure its features are accessible to all users, regardless of their physical or cognitive abilities.

4. Minimizing Harm

Ethical design seeks to minimize the potential harm that products can cause. In the case of WhatsApp, this could involve measures to prevent the spread of misinformation, hate speech, and harmful content.

5. Empowerment and Control

Users should have control over their digital experiences. Ethical design empowers users to customize their settings, manage their data, and make informed choices about their interactions on the platform.

The Drawbacks of WhatsApp

While WhatsApp has undoubtedly revolutionized communication, it is not without its drawbacks. These drawbacks highlight the need for ethical design and a user-centric approach:

1. Privacy Concerns

WhatsApp's data-sharing practices with its parent company, Facebook, have raised significant privacy concerns. Users have become increasingly wary of how their personal information is being used and shared across platforms.

2. Misinformation and Disinformation

The platform has been criticized for its role in facilitating the spread of misinformation, leading to real-world consequences. WhatsApp's end-to-end encryption, while protecting users' messages from interception, has also made it challenging to address the issue of false information.

3. User Experience and Accessibility

WhatsApp's design, though user-friendly for many, may not be fully accessible to individuals with disabilities. The lack of certain accessibility features can exclude a portion of the population from fully participating in digital communication.

4. Digital Well-being

Prolonged use of WhatsApp and similar platforms has been linked to digital addiction and reduced well-being. The constant notifications and the pressure to stay connected can contribute to increased stress and anxiety.

5. Monetization and Business Interests

WhatsApp's integration of business features, while offering new avenues for communication, also raises concerns about the balance between user experience and the pursuit of business interests.

Mitigating Drawbacks through Ethical Design and User-Centricity

1. Strengthening Privacy Measures

Ethical design demands that WhatsApp prioritize user privacy by implementing stringent data protection measures. This includes clear communication about data-sharing practices and providing users with the ability to opt out of certain data collection activities.

2. Combating Misinformation

A user-centric approach involves creating mechanisms within the platform to address the spread of false information. This could include collaborations with fact-checking organizations and the development of tools to flag and verify information.

3. Enhancing Accessibility

Ethical design requires WhatsApp to make its platform accessible to all users. This can be achieved through features such as voice commands, screen readers, and user interface adjustments to accommodate different needs.

4. Promoting Digital Well-being

Ethical design encourages WhatsApp to incorporate features that promote healthy digital habits. This could involve customizable notification settings, reminders for breaks, and tools that allow users to monitor and manage their screen time.

5. Balancing Monetization and User Experience

A user-centric approach necessitates finding a balance between business interests and user satisfaction. This could involve transparent communication about business-driven features and ensuring that they do not compromise the core user experience.

Conclusion

As WhatsApp continues to evolve, the importance of ethical design and user-centricity cannot be overstated. By prioritizing user well-being, privacy, and accessibility, WhatsApp can address many of the drawbacks associated with its platform. Ethical design goes beyond aesthetics and functionality; it is a commitment to creating a digital environment that enriches lives while upholding core values. As users, stakeholders, and designers, we have a shared responsibility to shape the evolution of WhatsApp and similar platforms in a way that benefits all of humanity.

Chapter 18. Toward Digital Responsibility

Introduction

In an era marked by the unprecedented growth of digital communication, the evolution of platforms like WhatsApp has reshaped the way we interact, share information, and connect with one another. As technology continually advances, it becomes increasingly vital to address the concept of digital responsibility - a guiding principle that shapes our behavior and engagement within these digital spaces. This article delves into the evolution of WhatsApp, highlights key takeaways concerning digital responsibility, and proposes a comprehensive roadmap for its prudent usage, with a focus on the roles of individuals, technology providers, and society at large.

The Evolution of WhatsApp

WhatsApp, once a humble messaging application, has undergone a remarkable transformation since its inception. Originally designed to facilitate real-time text communication, it now encompasses a plethora of features, including voice and video calls, multimedia sharing, group chats, and more. This evolution has granted users unprecedented convenience and connectivity, enabling them to bridge geographical gaps and maintain relationships across borders.

However, this evolution has also brought about a host of challenges related to digital responsibility. The ease of sharing information, coupled with the viral nature of content dissemination, demands a thoughtful approach to ensure that the power of communication is harnessed for the greater good.

Key Takeaways

1. Information Integrity and Fact-Checking: The rapid sharing of information can lead to the dissemination of false or misleading content. As responsible digital citizens, it is imperative to verify the accuracy of information before sharing it. Technology providers can play a pivotal role by integrating mechanisms for users to easily fact-check content within the platform.

2. Digital Footprint Awareness: Every interaction within digital spaces contributes to an individual's digital footprint. Whether it's a casual chat or a shared media file, these elements collectively shape one's online identity. Practicing discretion and understanding the implications of each digital action is central to fostering digital responsibility.

3. Cybersecurity and Privacy: With greater connectivity comes increased vulnerability. Users must be vigilant about safeguarding their personal information, utilizing strong passwords, and remaining cautious of potential phishing attempts. Similarly, technology providers must continually enhance security features and educate users about potential risks.

4. Mindful Content Sharing: The instantaneous nature of messaging platforms like WhatsApp can sometimes lead to thoughtless sharing of sensitive or inappropriate content. Exercising mindfulness in content sharing is a cornerstone of digital responsibility, promoting a positive and respectful online environment.

A Roadmap for Responsible WhatsApp Usage

1. Individual Empowerment and Education

> ➤ Understand the platform: Users should acquaint themselves with WhatsApp's features and settings to make informed choices about their online presence.
> ➤ Media literacy: Education about identifying and questioning misleading information can empower users to become critical consumers of digital content.
> ➤ Privacy awareness: Individuals should actively manage their privacy settings and be cautious about sharing personal details.

2. Technological Innovations for Responsibility

> ➤ Fact-checking integration: WhatsApp and other technology providers can collaborate with reputable fact-checking organizations to seamlessly verify information before it is shared.
> ➤ Safety prompts: Implementing prompts that encourage users to reconsider sharing potentially harmful content can contribute to a more thoughtful online discourse.
> ➤ User-friendly security features: Enhancing security protocols, two-factor authentication, and encryption mechanisms can bolster user confidence.

3. Collective Responsibility of Society

> ➤ Digital citizenship education: Educational institutions and community organizations can incorporate digital responsibility into their curricula, fostering responsible behavior from a young age.

➢ Ethical guidelines for content creation: **Content creators, influencers, and businesses should adhere to ethical standards when using platforms like WhatsApp to reach their audience.**

➢ Public awareness campaigns: **Collaborative efforts by governments, NGOs, and technology companies can raise awareness about responsible digital behavior and its broader societal impact.**

Conclusion

As WhatsApp continues to evolve, the concept of digital responsibility emerges as a vital compass to navigate the complexities of the digital realm. Embracing digital responsibility requires a concerted effort from individuals, technology providers, and society at large. By fostering a culture of mindful content sharing, fact-checking, cybersecurity awareness, and ethical behavior, we can collectively harness the power of WhatsApp for positive and constructive interactions. The roadmap outlined in this article serves as a foundation upon which a more digitally responsible future can be built, where the benefits of connectivity are maximized, and the challenges are met with wisdom and integrity. In this interconnected world, the journey toward digital responsibility is a journey toward a more harmonious and empowered global community.

"WhatsApp Evolution and Digital Responsibility" is a comprehensive exploration of the transformative journey undertaken by communication platforms, with a focus on the paradigm-shifting evolution of WhatsApp. This illuminating book navigates the historical landscape of communication technologies, tracing the trailblazing path that led to WhatsApp's meteoric rise. It delves into the instant communication revolution ignited by WhatsApp, reshaping interpersonal connections and transcending geographical confines. From dismantling borders to impacting global economies through its cost-effective messaging model, WhatsApp's dynamic influence is dissected.

The book critically analyzes the psychological ramifications of perpetual connectivity, while dissecting the intricate web of misinformation propagation and its societal repercussions. With an incisive lens on privacy issues, group dynamics, and hate speech, this book champions the cultivation of digital literacy and healthy online habits. Drawing from a rich tapestry of insights, it offers pragmatic strategies for responsible WhatsApp usage, steering towards an inclusive, ethical, and user-centric digital future.

ABOUT THE AUTHOR

Mr. C. P. Kumar is a retired Scientist 'G' from National Institute of Hydrology, Roorkee, Uttarakhand, India. He is also a Reiki Healer and Chakra Balancing practitioner (with pendulum dowsing) and offers Emotional Freedom Technique (EFT) to help individuals with emotional issues. Mr. Kumar has authored many books on technical, spiritual, and social topics.

For further details, you may visit his webpage
https://www.angelfire.com/nh/cpkumar/virgo.html